# Frustrated, Angry and Mad

## Adrian Laurent

Copyright © 2022 by Adrian Laurent. Bradem Press, New Zealand.
ISBN 978-1-99-117482-6, (EPUB), 978-1-99-117480-2 (Paperback)

All rights reserved. No part of this book may be reproduced or used in any manner without written permission of the copyright owner except for the use of quotations in a book review. This is a work of fiction. Names, characters, places, and incidents either are the product of the author's imagination or are used fictitiously. Any resemblance to actual persons, living or dead, events, or locales is entirely coincidental Although the publisher and the author have made every effort to ensure that the information in this book was correct at press time and while this publication is designed to provide accurate information in regard to the subject matter covered, the publisher and the author assume no responsibility for errors, inaccuracies, omissions, or any other inconsistencies herein and hereby disclaim any liability to any party for any loss, damage, or disruption caused by errors or omissions, whether such errors or omissions result from negligence, accident, or any other cause. The information in this book is not intended to be used, nor should be used, to diagnose or treat any mental health or medical condition. For diagnosis or treatment of any mental health or medical condition, consult a licensed professional, psychologist or physician. Both the author and publisher of this book are not liable or responsible for any damages or negative consequences from any preparation, treatment, action, application to any person.

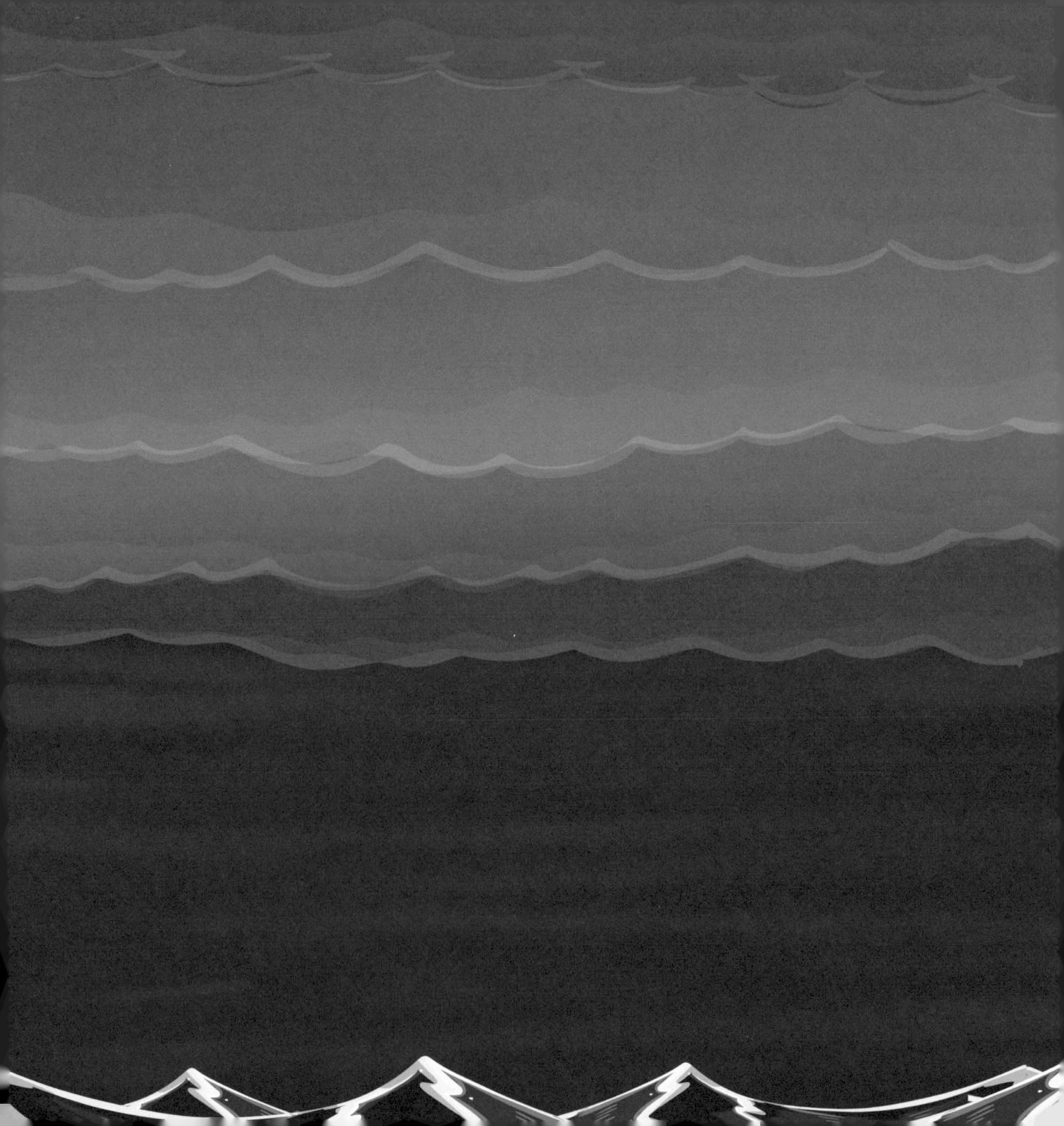

# This Book Belongs to:

Parker loved playing with dinosaurs. Super T-Rex prepared to blast into space to defeat the Evil Triceratops. But T-Rex needed a rocket. Where could Parker's rocket be?

Parker found his little brother Jordan playing with the rocket in his bedroom. Parker wanted it and sharing is hard. He started to feel angry. His face felt hot. His heart beat faster. His muscles felt tight.

Parker knew it helped to move away from what made him angry. He walked back to the living room and sat on the floor but still felt angry. How could he help the anger go away?

Suddenly Parker heard a voice. He looked down and saw T-Rex looking up at him and frowning.
"Wow!" Said T-Rex, "You look angry. Everybody feels angry sometimes, especially T-Rexs! But I know how to control anger before it explodes."

"Most of the time we feel calm and relaxed. This is when our anger is low. Our body and head feel relaxed like a still ocean. Our breathing and heart feel normal. Our muscles are soft. But things can make us feel angry. Everyone feels angry sometimes, but if our anger gets big we can feel like shouting, hitting and breaking. It's OK to feel angry but not OK to hurt people or break things," said T-Rex.

"If we don't control our anger it can become so big we lose control. It's like a stormy sea with strong winds and crashing waves. When we feel angry our head feels fuzzy and muscles are tight. Our breathing and heart are faster. But I know 4 ways that can help control anger before it explodes," said T-Rex.

"First notice how you feel. How does your breathing and heart beat feel? Is your head clear or cloudy? Are your muscles tight or relaxed?" said T-Rex.

"Next, get some space. That's what you did when you came into this room. Well done! It feels better to be away from what makes you angry," said T-Rex.

"Next, take 10 deep breaths," said T-Rex. "Breath in deeply through your nose and out through your mouth." Parker counted 10 deep breaths. He felt his anger shrink, but he didn't feel calm yet.

"Then move your body," said T-Rex.
Parker jumped up and down. He ran on the spot. T-Rex did jumping jacks. Then he squeezed all his muscles and let them go.

Finally, he felt his anger shrink down. He felt calm. His breathing slowed. His head felt clear. The stormy sea was still and gentle again.

Parker went back to his bedroom. Jordan held out T-Rex.
"Shall we play together?" Asked Jordan.
Parker nodded and took T-Rex with a smile.
"Let's fly T-Rex to space together," said Parker.
T-Rex flew around the Moon and landed on Mars. They played happily until dinner, but Evil Triceratops got away, for now!

I hope you enjoyed the story.

Feedback from fantastic readers like you helps other parents find this book and give them confidence to choose it.

I would be so grateful if you could take one minute to click the link below or scan the QR code and leave your feedback:

Leave a review on Amazon.com (US)

or Amazon.co.uk (UK)

Thank you!

With Love,

Adrian Laurent

Download free activity sheets
and helpful resources for this book.

Click Here
or scan the QR code below:

With Love,

Adrian Laurent

Collect the whole series and
learn essential social emotional life skills.

Click HERE or scan the QR code to discover more:

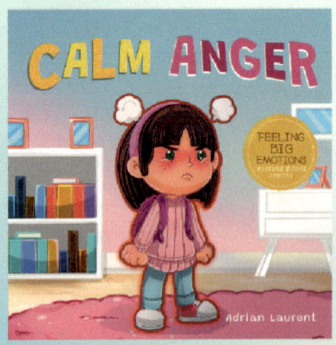
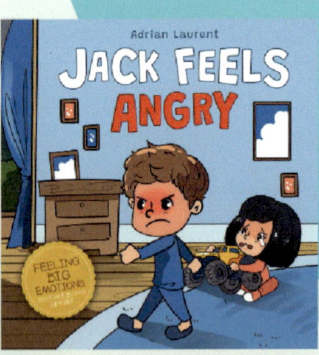
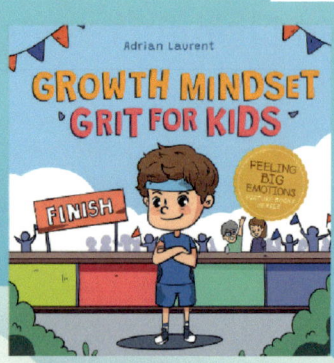
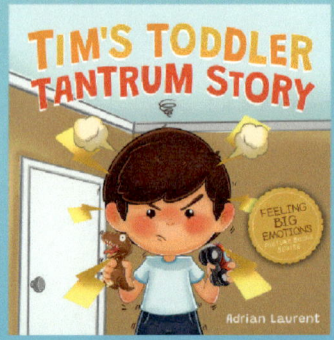

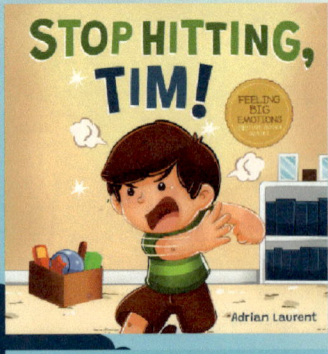

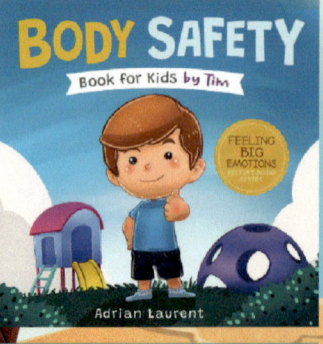
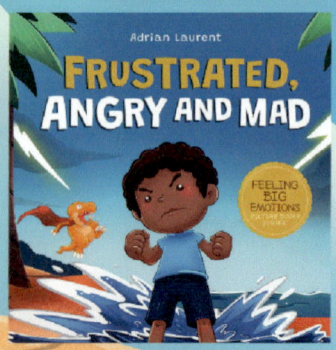

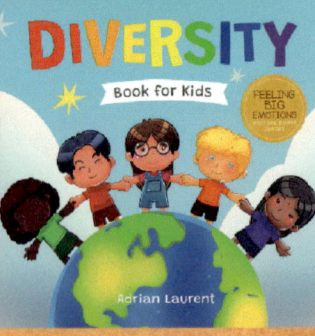
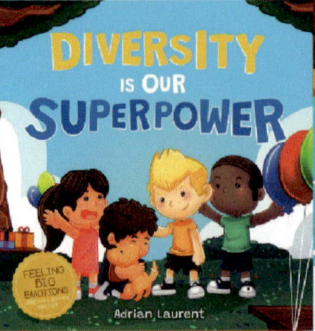
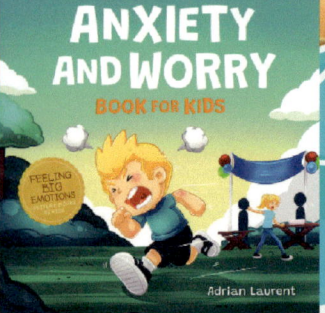

Made in the USA
Columbia, SC
31 August 2024